Jobs
and Work People Do

By
Émilie Gorostis

Illustrated by
Pierre Caillou
Hélène Convert
Jean-Sébastien Deheeger
Christian Guibbaud

Twirl

Contents

Index 92

The "Let's Review!" pages at the end of each section help reinforce learning.

Index Quickly find the word you're looking for with the index at the end of the book.

Look for the colored boxes in the bottom right-hand corners. You will find references to related subjects in other parts of the book.

What Is a Job?

Jobs

You might have heard grown-ups talking about their jobs. But what *is* a job?

These jobs are big dreams, but they don't exist.

knight:
fights dragons

superhero:
rescues people

Santa Claus:
gives out presents

These jobs are big dreams, and they do exist.

slide tester

panda nanny

toy brick builder

A job is a position or task that an employer—the person or company that hired you—pays you to do. The job may be something that you have been trained to do or are very good at doing.

SCHOOL

learn

employer

look for work

cabinetmaker

work

receive payment

Many people around the world vote for their country's president, or leader, in an election.

The job of being president is very demanding. That person's mission is to make the best decisions to help the people of the country.

You might have a job or mission at school to help others in your class, such as handing out snacks or putting away books. That's important too!

🖌 In a House

A home that needs repairs or renovations requires many types of craftspeople.

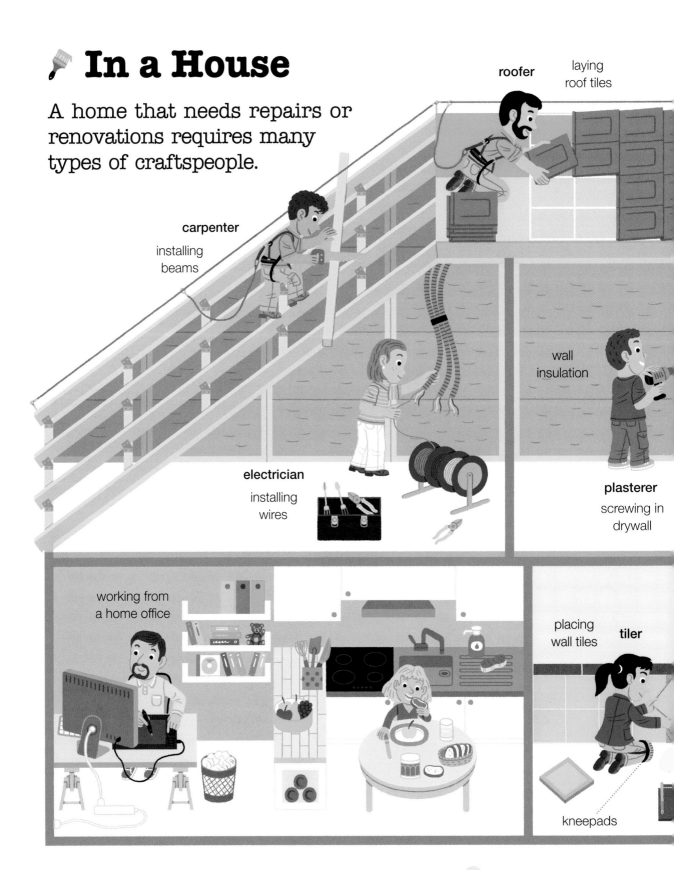

roofer
laying roof tiles

carpenter
installing beams

wall insulation

electrician
installing wires

plasterer
screwing in drywall

working from a home office

placing wall tiles   **tiler**

kneepads

joiner
putting in windows

house painter
painting walls

plumbing and heating specialist
installing water pipes

mason
building a cinder block wall

trowel

What
work can be done from home ?

In the morning, you leave the house to go to school. Your parents may go to work in an office or outside.

But there are people who work where they live. For example, some day care providers take care of babies and young children in their own homes.

With technology, it is common nowadays to work from home. It is called working remotely. People can have meetings with their coworkers online.

In the Morning **12**
Designing Toys **32**

# In the Morning

Many people start their work early in the day, before you leave for school.

arborist

pruning trees

figuring out the best use for land

creating a vertical garden wall

landscaper

NEW PLAYGROUND COMING

urban planner

garbage truck driver

picking up and removing trash

garbage collectors

movers

moving boxes
and furniture

**sanitation
worker**

vacuuming
trash

**traffic
officer**

monitoring parking
violations

taking passengers
where they want
to go

TAXI

taxi driver

newsstand vendor

selling newspapers
and magazines

**school bus
driver**

driving
children
to school

leak hunter

detecting
leaky pipes

Where
does the garbage truck go

?

Garbage collectors might empty trash cans early in the morning or late at night.

The trash is taken to a processing center, where workers sort out the recyclable waste. Waste that can't be recycled is taken to landfills.

Some cities have special waste disposal areas. You can take things like old appliances, tires, car batteries, and paint to these sites.

In a School

Teachers aren't the only professionals who work at a school.

interactive digital whiteboard

5 X 3 =

teaching math

librarian

elementary school teacher

setting out books for students

computer technician

fixing computers

administrative assistant

principal

providing information

welcoming a new family

Computer Lab

music teacher

maintenance worker

classroom aid

installing coatracks

attending to a sick child

directing the choir

art teacher — planning a craft project

food service worker — preparing meals

Staff Lounge

teacher's assistant — supervising recess

crossing guard — helping students cross the street safely

Before a new school year begins, your parents help you prepare by getting you a backpack and school supplies. Your teachers have to get ready too.

All the teachers usually meet with the principal about two weeks before the first day of school.

Your teachers have to set up the classrooms, organize the textbooks and supplies, and plan the lessons.

A Classroom Aide's Day

A classroom aide helps a preschool or kindergarten teacher in class, during lunch, and on the playground.

morning

setting up the toys

discussing lesson plans with the teacher

welcoming the children

working with students on an activity

wiping a child's nose

midday

taking children to the bathroom

showing children how to wash their hands

helping at lunchtime

Who
cooks the meals in the cafeteria ?

afternoon

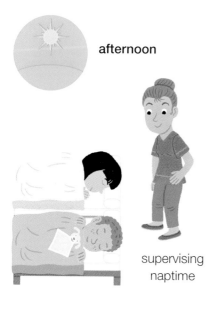

supervising naptime

tying shoelaces

watching children at recess

evening

tidying the classroom

cleaning up

helping with homework

When you eat in the cafeteria, a food service worker serves you food.

At some schools, there may be a chef who prepares the meals in the school kitchen.

In larger school districts, meals can be prepared in a central kitchen and then delivered to several schools.

In a School **14**
At a Restaurant **78**

AB Teaching

Are you good at explaining how things work?
Do you like showing people how something is done?
You might like being a teacher!

Preschool

Elementary School

geography

reading

math

music

preschool teacher: teaches children
basic skills and concepts

**elementary school
teacher:** teaches
several subjects

Middle School and High School

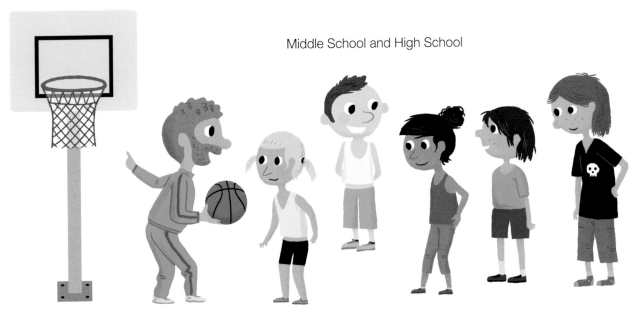

middle and high school teacher:
teaches a specific subject

Vocational School

apprenticeship supervisor: teaches a specific skill

apprentice

College or University

professor, who may also be a **researcher**

students

You go to school to learn so you can have a job when you grow up. But why do some grown-ups go to school when they already have jobs?

Grown-ups may take training courses to learn new things to be better at their current jobs. They might learn a different computer system or language!

They may also take classes in order to change jobs. Lots of people change jobs a few times in their lives!

Helping People

There are times when we need help from professionals in special fields. These people are well trained to provide care.

speech therapist: helps children speak clearly and easily

psychologist: helps children voice their feelings

psychomotor therapist: helps children improve their movement and balance skills

special education paraprofessional: provides children with extra learning support

accompanying
a disabled child
to recess

special education
aide

special education
teacher

planning activities to help students express themselves

When some parents decide to divorce, a family mediator can help them communicate better.

Lawyers explain the steps that parents take in order to divorce. The lawyers for each parent will speak for them in front of the family court judge.

When parents can't agree on certain things, the judge will choose what they feel is best for the family.

Making Books

The books you read at home or at school are created by many people who work together to bring you exciting stories.

sketches

creating the images based on the story

drawing tablet

illustrator

coming up with an idea and writing the story

author

Publishing House

working with the author to shape the story

editor

choosing the illustrator

planning the format of the book

putting the words and pictures together on the pages

designer

correcting errors

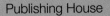

copy editor

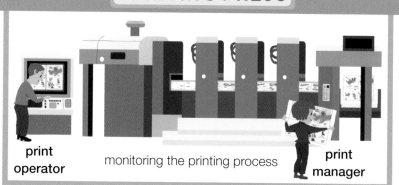

PRINTING PRESS

print operator

monitoring the printing process

print manager

promoting the book

publicist

presenting the book to booksellers

sales representative

BOOKSTORE

bookseller

SIGNING

organizing a book signing

window display selling books

How
do you become an author ?

You may have a great imagination and love to make up stories. These are important qualities if you decide to become an author.

You also need to keep coming up with story ideas and practice writing all the time.

When your story is finished, you might send it to a literary agent, who will help you find a publisher interested in turning your story into a book!

In a House **10**
Shopping District **58**

Let's Review!

Match each image with the names of the jobs. Do you know what each person does in their job?

taxi driver   traffic officer   sanitation worker   arborist   urban planner

The classroom aide is busy all day. What are some of the tasks this aide does?
Match the labels to the correct image.

setting up
the toys

welcoming
the children

tying
shoelaces

helping with
homework

A copy editor pays careful attention to details and is able to spot mistakes.
Can you see what's different between these two pictures? Look closely—there are seven differences!

teacher

panda nanny

designer

There are many jobs that
you can do in the future.
Which of these shown here might
you like to do? Why?

food service worker

roofer

school bus driver

Recreation

♞ Equestrian Center

Working at a riding center is a dream come true for people who love horses.

horse van

director of the center

ordering food and supplies

stable hand

braiding a mane

breeder

helping the horse deliver her foal

barn manager

demonstrating grooming

groom

cleaning a stall

food buckets

riding instructor

giving a lesson

professional rider

competition coach

administering a vaccine

veterinarian

medical supplies

replacing a horseshoe

treating the horse's back problem

farrier

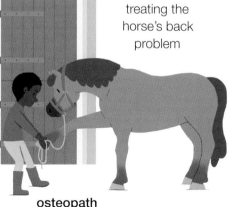

osteopath

Have you ever had a toothache? Horses can have them too. The part of a horse's bridle in its mouth, called a bit, can sometimes hurt them.

When that happens, it's time to call an equine dentist! This person is a veterinarian who specializes in dental care for horses.

The dentist uses an equine mouth speculum to keep the horse's mouth open, then files down its damaged teeth with an electric tooth file.

Soccer Stadium

Playing professional soccer is a job! There are also many jobs related to the sport.

exercising to strengthen muscles

professional soccer player

supervising warm-ups

fitness trainer

explaining game strategies

coach

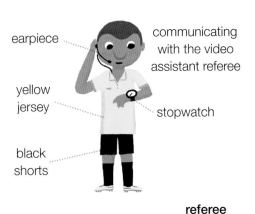

earpiece

communicating with the video assistant referee

yellow jersey

stopwatch

black shorts

referee

warning a player by showing a yellow card

waving a flag to signal game action to the referee

assistant referee

negotiating contracts
for players

**sports
agent**

looking for new
players

**sports
scout**

conducting
an interview

**sports
reporter**

You may have heard of soccer
players who earn lots of
money—enough to buy and
drive a different car every day
for a year!

training young
players

youth coach

Professional soccer teams often
pay a lot of money to get the
best soccer players to play for
them.

treating
injuries

attending to
injured players

cold spray
treatment

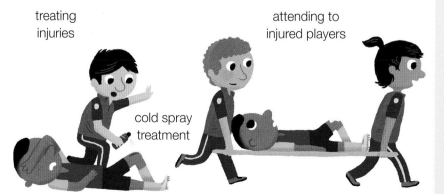

physiotherapist

sports medicine physicians

Popular soccer stars can also
earn money off the field by
appearing at events or in
advertisements.

Designing Toys

It takes teams of people to come up with and make the toys everyone loves to play with.

Research Department

designers

creating a 3-D model

sketching a design

choosing the materials and colors

3-D printer

making a prototype

band saw

wood lathe

Workshop

craftspeople

drill

painting

applying varnish

Factory

plastic injection molding machine

worker

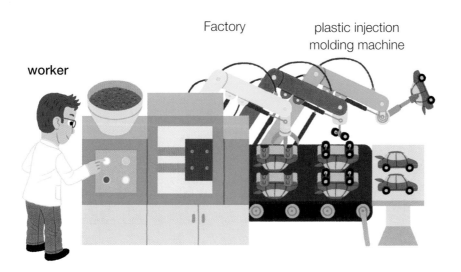

Laboratory

technician

toy testers

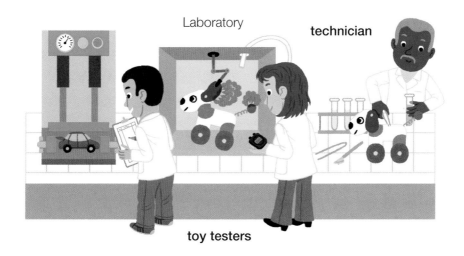

Toy Store

owner

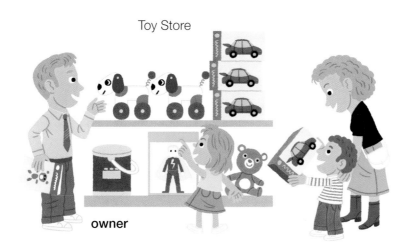

🎭 Theater

Let's put on a show! Actors, costume designers, sound technicians, and many others work together to create memorable performances.

stage designer
building scenery

Stage Wings

stagehand
moving props to change the set

trapeze

trapeze artist

Stage

costume designer
creating a costume

sound technician
monitoring equipment volum

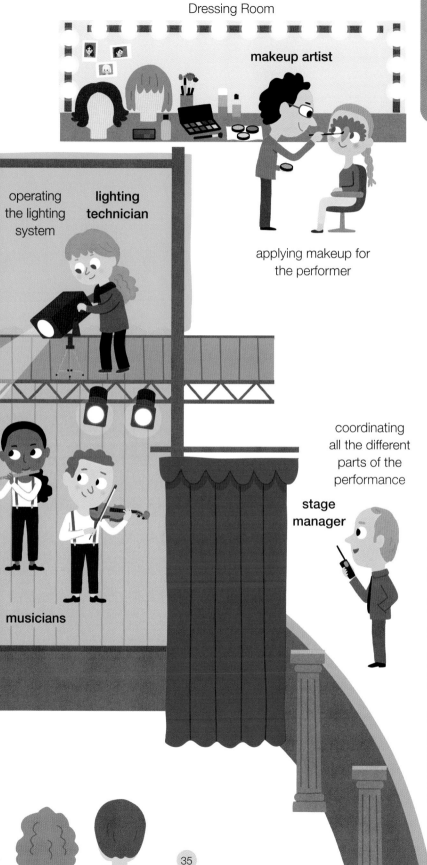

Dressing Room

makeup artist

operating the lighting system

lighting technician

applying makeup for the performer

musicians

coordinating all the different parts of the performance

stage manager

Trapeze artists make swinging and hanging from a trapeze look so easy. But, as with all circus performers, they have to practice their act for a long time.

In the past, circus performers learned the job from their parents. It was a family business!

Today there are schools where you can learn to become a professional circus artist.

An Orchestra Conductor's Day

The conductor guides the orchestra musicians to produce the best representation of a musical piece.

morning
day of the concert

afternoon
dress rehearsal

reviewing a piece
of music

playing the
music to get
a feel for it

using a baton to
conduct the orchestra

listening
to music

getting
dressed

doing breathing
exercises to relax

evening
during the concert

keeping time for . . .

slow music

lively music

dreamy music · angry music

closing his eyes · frowning

---

night
after the concert

meeting the
audience

relaxing with the musicians

traveling to the next
concert venue

There are jobs that have been traditionally held by men, but more and more women are being hired for those positions.

While there are still not many women conductors, they can be found in orchestras around the world.

Changing people's beliefs about which jobs can be held by women or by men will take time. It's important to not let those beliefs keep you from the job you want.

Theater **34**

Museum

The natural history museum is a great place for people who are interested in science-related jobs.

curator

planning the museum's exhibits

greeter

welcoming visitors and telling them about special exhibits

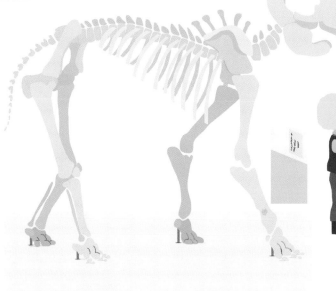

tour guide

telling visitors how scientists put together animal skeletons

education coordinator

showing replicas of dinosaur bones

security officer

registrar   keeping track of the museum's collection

Do you love learning about
dinosaurs? Perhaps you would like
to be a paleontologist, a scientist
who studies fossils and the
remains of prehistoric animals.

conservator

taxidermist

preparing animal
bodies for display

making sure
items stay in
good condition

Together with other scientists
and researchers, some
paleontologists go on digs to
uncover long-buried dinosaur
bones.

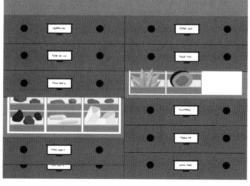

restorer

minerals

The paleontologists will carefully
wrap up the bones and bring
them back to their laboratory
for further study.

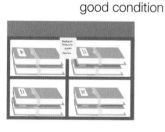

mineralogist

studying
mineral
samples

dusting the dried
plant specimens

These are jobs at an equestrian center. Can you describe what each person does?

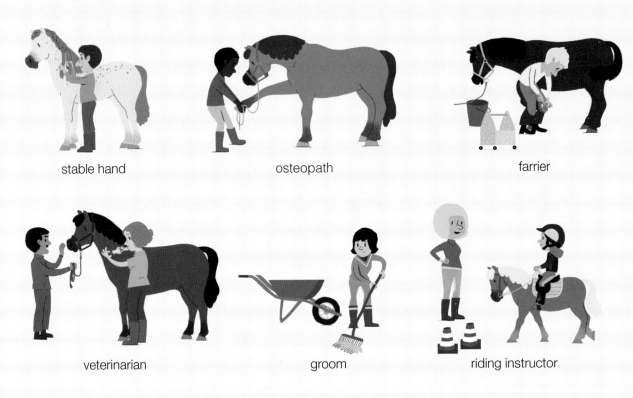

stable hand

osteopath

farrier

veterinarian

groom

riding instructor

Name the jobs at this toy workshop.

What does each person do? Can you name some of the tools they use?

Animal skeletons are rebuilt at natural history museums.
Can you connect the missing bones to where they belong on this mammoth?

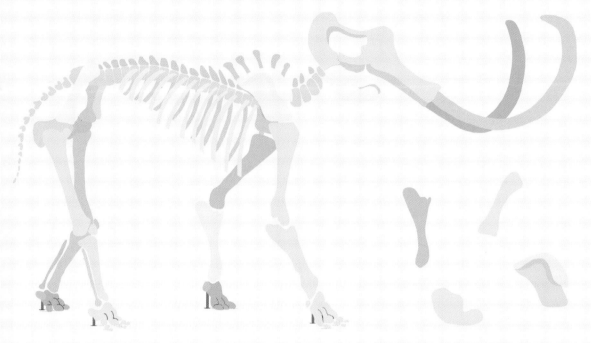

Whose job was it to dig up the bones of this prehistoric creature?
Do you see yourself doing something like this? Why or why not?

Some jobs require leading a group of people.
What jobs do these people have?
What do you think they have to do to make sure people work together?

Medical and Rescue Workers

An Accident

It's an emergency! Some skiers got hurt on the mountain, and help arrives quickly.

ski patroller

putting up warning signs

Hospital

rescue sled

evacuating injured people

ski patroller

EMERGENCY

driving quickly and carefully

ambulance driver

rescue
helicopter

avalanche

emergency
medical
technician

administering
first aid

rescue dog
and handler

searching for
trapped skiers

What
do you do when there's an accident?

When an accident occurs, someone calls the emergency services number right away. In the United States and Canada, this number is 911.

The emergency dispatcher asks questions such as: What is the location of the accident? How did it happen? Where is the person hurt?

This information is important so the first responders know what to do when they arrive. The injured person can be taken care of quickly.

A Firefighter's Day

Many firefighters work long hours,
and the firehouse is their second home.

morning

exercising

mannequin

training with a partner

eating with other firefighters

afternoon

pager

making sure the station's
vehicle is running well

alternate response
vehicle

going out
on a call

gurney

How
do firefighters rescue animals ?

night

relaxing while waiting
for a call

Sleeping Quarters

waking up to go
on a call

fire tanker truck

putting out a trash fire

morning

going home

resting before
the next shift

Not only do firefighters save the lives of people, but they also often come to the rescue of animals, like a cat that got stuck in a tree.

Firefighters can help animals in danger: pets that are trapped in a burning house, a horse stuck in mud, and many other situations.

Firefighters will even get rid of a hornet nest if it might be dangerous to the public.

An Accident **44**
Children's Hospital **48**

✚ Children's Hospital

Here you will find kids who are taken care of by professionals in many different departments.

nurse

giving medicine

medical administrative assistants

greeting visitors

handling billing

analyzing blood samples

medical technologist

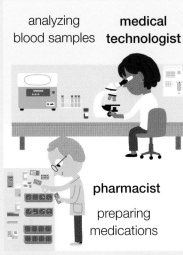

pharmacist

preparing medications

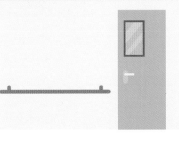

performing a scan to detect injury

radiologist

hospital cleaner

washing skin and taking temperatures

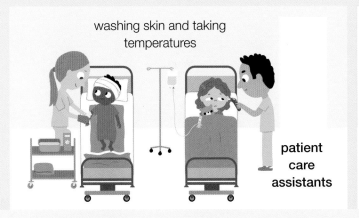

patient care assistants

providing pregnancy care

midwife

laundry worker

washing and ironing hospital laundry

preparing meals for staff and patients

cook

dietician

planning nutritious meals

entertainer

teacher

caring for newborn babies

pediatric nurse

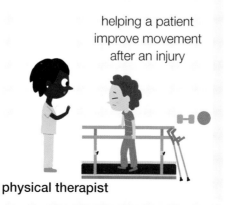

helping a patient improve movement after an injury

physical therapist

How
do you become a doctor ?

You may have a toy medical kit and enjoy pretending to be a doctor. Maybe you use a toy stethoscope to listen to your stuffed bear's heartbeat.

If you enjoy finding out how the human body works, perhaps being a doctor is for you. It takes many years of studying and hard work.

After finishing medical school, the graduates work at hospitals and clinics. They need more training if they decide to specialize in a field of medicine.

Operating Room **50**
Special Doctors **52**

✂ Operating Room

Surgery is also known as an operation. Surgeons are doctors who use special tools to fix problems on or inside the body.

surgeon

preparing for surgery by washing her hands thoroughly

tray

surgical light

lancets

needle and thread

compresses

retractor

stapler

surgical nurse

disinfecting the skin

anesthesiologist

providing medicine that will put the patient to sleep until the surgery is over

electrodes

anesthesia mask

electrocardiogram: monitors heart activity and tracks breathing

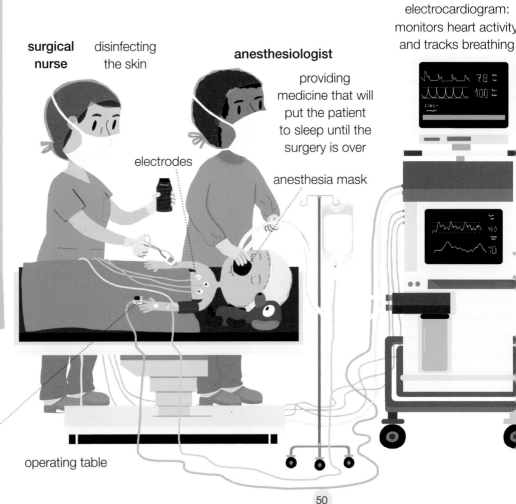

pulse oximeter: measures amount of oxygen in the blood

operating table

surgical cap

mask

gloves

surgical gown

scrubs

surgical clogs

surgeon preparing
to operate

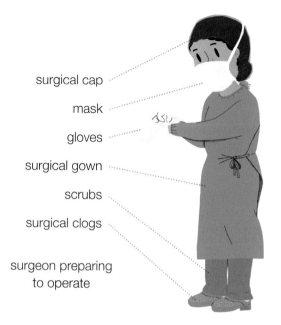

When you paint, you wear a smock to protect your clothes. In an operating room, a surgeon wears a surgical gown to keep the patient safe from bacteria.

Surgical gowns and other protective clothing also protect the surgical team from blood or chemical spills that might happen during surgery.

The instruments that the surgeons use are also sterilized. All these measures are taken to ensure a clean and safe environment.

after the operation

orderly

taking the patient
to their room

nurse

checking the
patient's condition

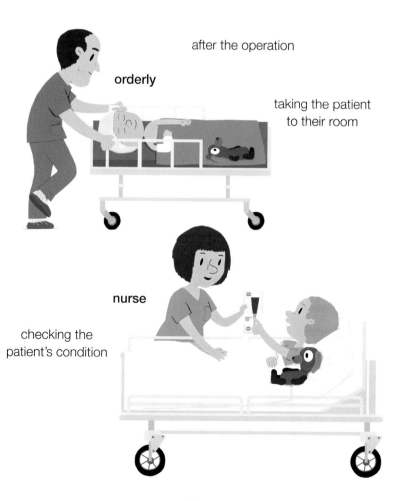

♪ Special Doctors

The first doctor you see when you don't feel well is your primary care doctor. If the illness requires specific care, you may need to see a specialist.

Medical Clinic

Waiting Room

asking questions

primary care doctor

blood pressure monitor

stethoscope

listening to the heart and lungs

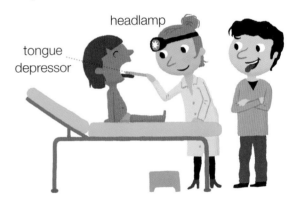

headlamp

tongue depressor

checking the throat for redness or swelling

prescribing medicine

giving special instructions for care

tests vision

prescribes glasses

treats ear infections

tests hearing

biomicroscope

ophthalmologist

otoscope

ear, nose, and throat specialist

eyes

nose
ears
throat

teeth

skin

dentist

dermatologist

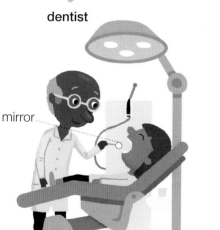

mirror

dermatoscope

checks your teeth and gums

applying skin cream

What
is a pediatrician ?

Doctors who specialize in care for children are called pediatricians. Their patients are teenagers, young children, and even newborns!

The pediatrician knows all about the changes a child goes through as they grow. They understand childhood issues and can explain what to expect at each stage.

There are specialists for elderly people too. Geriatricians help patients take care of themselves as they age.

Children's Hospital **48**
Operating Room **50**

Let's Review!

If there is an accident on the ski slopes, you might see ski patrollers, a rescue dog handler, an ambulance driver, and an emergency medical technician. Locate each one, then follow the path with your finger to review what they do.

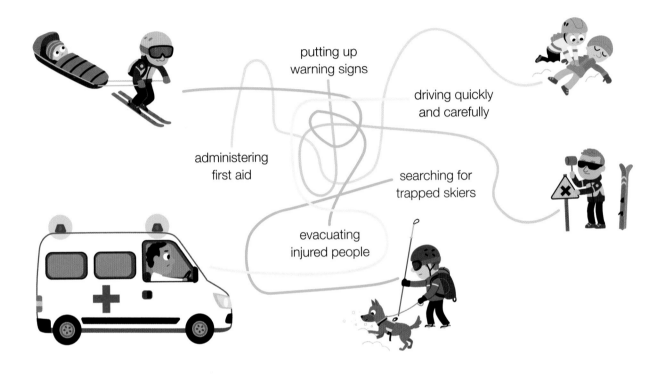

putting up
warning signs

driving quickly
and carefully

administering
first aid

searching for
trapped skiers

evacuating
injured people

Point to the people who work at a hospital. Do you know the names of their jobs? What jobs do the others have?

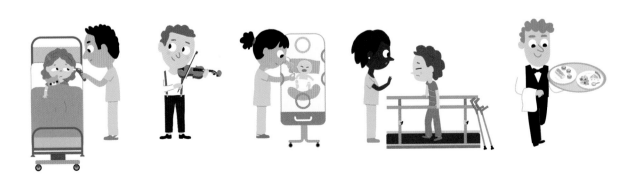

lancets

needle and thread

compresses

retractor

stapler

The surgeon is preparing to operate on a patient. She has to have all her instruments available. Place them in the correct place on the cart.

The surgeon is wearing special clothing. Can you name each piece?

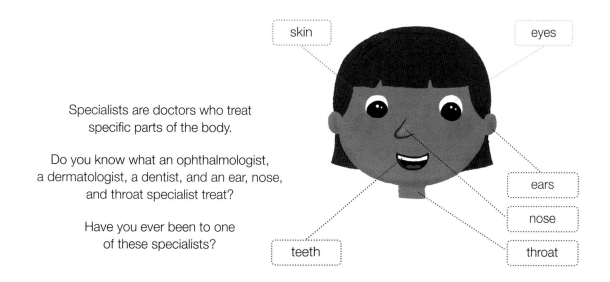

skin

eyes

Specialists are doctors who treat specific parts of the body.

Do you know what an ophthalmologist, a dermatologist, a dentist, and an ear, nose, and throat specialist treat?

Have you ever been to one of these specialists?

ears

nose

throat

teeth

Making and Selling Products

Shopping District

Stores are often located together in the middle of towns and cities. Here, many people provide services or sell products.

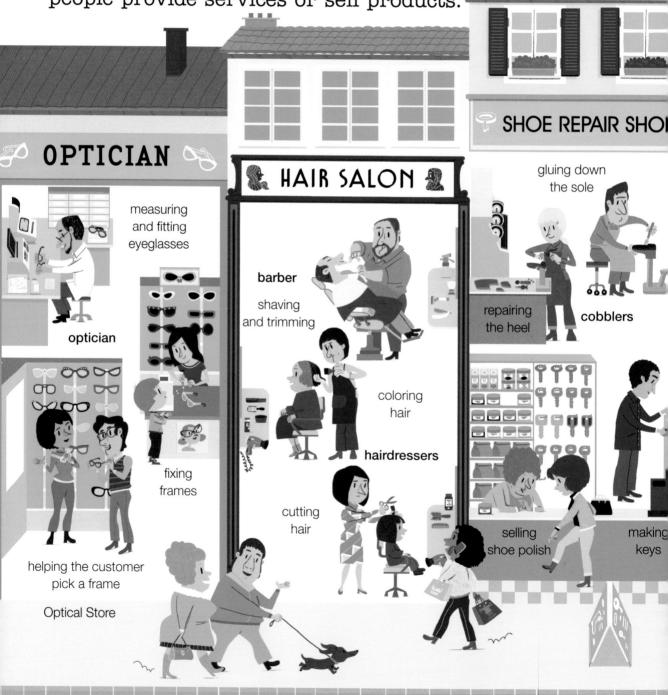

OPTICIAN

measuring and fitting eyeglasses

optician

fixing frames

helping the customer pick a frame

Optical Store

HAIR SALON

barber

shaving and trimming

coloring hair

hairdressers

cutting hair

SHOE REPAIR SHO

gluing down the sole

repairing the heel

cobblers

selling shoe polish

making keys

store clerk

organizing the
clothing rack

Clothing Store

CLOTHES 4 U

creating the
window display

...ning the
...tal gate

Cold Room

removing
dry leaves

making
a bouquet

florists

FLOWER SHOP

taking orders

watering
the plants

Where
do flower shops get their flowers ?

You may have bought a bouquet of flowers for Mother's Day at the flower shop. It was probably hard to choose the prettiest bunch!

Florist

The flowers sold at the shop can come from flower farms all over the world. The Netherlands is the largest producer of tulips, about two billion a year!

Florists buy flowers for their shop at a special market, or they can order them online and have fresh flowers delivered.

Flower Market

Post Office

Workers at the post office have lots to do! They sell stamps, help you apply for a passport, and sort and deliver the mail.

processing passport applications

counter clerk

selling stamps and money orders

postal worker

teaching customers to use a self-service machine

providing information

sorting the letters
by street and
house number

sorting agent

getting ready
to deliver the
mail

collecting
mail from the
mailbox

mail carriers

Where
does the money in an ATM come from **?**

ATM stands for "automated teller machine." People withdraw money from an ATM using a debit or credit card. The money seems to appear almost like magic!

But it is not magic. Money in ATMs at banks are refilled by bank staff. Small businesses that have ATMs can hire a company to do it for them.

Did you know that there are more than 3 million ATMs in the world? There's even one in Antarctica!

Farmers Market

Local farmers regularly bring their produce and homemade goods to these markets around the city.

fruit and vegetable seller

paper bag

weighing the fruit

weighing scale

crates

fish vendors

scraping off fish scales

opening an oyster with an oyster knife

slicing a fish

gloves

scales

ice

boots

waterproof apron

Stall

Cheese Shop

thermometer

cheesemonger

using a cheese wire to slice cheese

taking a sample

refrigerated truck

Meat Shop

meat slicer

cleaver

butcher

grinding meat

Who
makes fish sticks

Fish sticks are popular around the world. They are made in factories that cut frozen fish into small "sticks," then coat them with a breadcrumb batter.

After they're fried and packaged, the frozen fish sticks are delivered to supermarkets. Fish vendors, on the other hand, sell freshly caught fish.

The just-caught fish are packed in ice to keep the fish fresh. Which do you enjoy eating: fish sticks or fresh fish?

Supermarket **66**
In the Country **84**

A Baker's Day

The baker is up really early to make bread and pastries. You can buy them when you wake up!

night

washing
his hands

taking the dough out
of the proofing box

starting a fire in
the brick oven

baking in the
electric oven

filling the baskets

morning

preparing the dough
for the next day

kneading
machine

dividing
the dough
into equal
portions

shaping
the dough

allowing the
dough to rest

afternoon

evening

Where
do some bakers live ?

cleaning

relaxing

filling out office paperwork

setting the alarm clock

going to bed early

At four o'clock in the morning, it's still dark out and you're fast asleep. But bakers are already at work!

In order to get to work quickly and easily, some bakers live where they work, right above the bakery.

Many small bakeries are family businesses. Some members work in the kitchen, while others work in the store.

BAKERY

Shopping District **58** 🏢
At a Restaurant **78** 🍽

🛒 Supermarket

Supermarkets are organized and well-stocked stores where you can find many kinds of food: cereals, vegetables, dairy products, and much more!

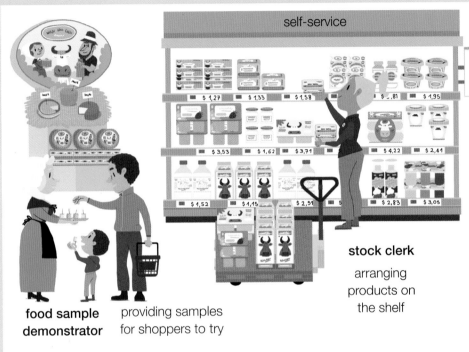

self-service

stock clerk

arranging products on the shelf

food sample demonstrator

providing samples for shoppers to try

BUY 2 GET 1 FREE

$ 4,67 $ 3,91 $ 2,92 $ 5,12 $ 3,58

$ 1,85 $ 3,75 $ 3,22 $ 3,14 $ 2,81 $ 5,   ,17

$ 4,58 $ 3,61   4 $ 3,75 $ 2,64 $ 2

scanner

department manager

ordering products from the warehouse

assistant manager

putting up a sign

store manager

signing for a delivery order

customer service assistant

answering shoppers' questions

anti-theft gate

helping shoppers use the machines

security guard

checkout assistant

safes

self-service checkout

cashier

scanning products and collecting payment

conveyor belt

bookkeeper

keeping track of daily sales

Waiting in a checkout line—especially a long line—is not fun. Many supermarkets have been looking for ways to cut down the wait time.

In some stores, customers scan the barcodes of the products as they shop. This method lets shoppers pay digitally using their phones.

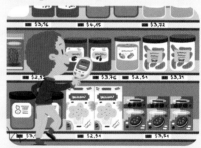

While this will allow shoppers to avoid waiting in long checkout lines, it does mean that cashiers will have to look for work elsewhere.

SUPERMARKET

⌨ Online Shopping

Today it is very common to shop online rather than make a trip to the store. Modern technology allows us to buy things, not just locally, but also from around the world. Who makes all this happen?

House

Web Design Company

web designer
designing a website

web developer
building a website using computer code

photographer
taking pictures of a product

order picker finding the right product

delivering
the package

**delivery
driver**

istribution Center

A drone can be a remote-controlled toy, but it is also a flying robot, able to lift things into the air.

Electrical engineers are working on technology for drones to deliver packages around the world.

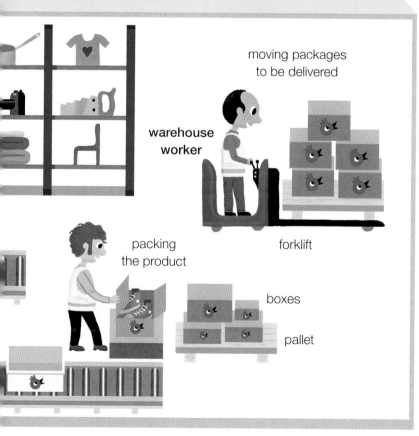

moving packages
to be delivered

**warehouse
worker**

forklift

packing
the product

boxes

pallet

Drones are operated by drone pilots, who can work for film companies, farms, the military, or even government agencies that want to deliver medical supplies.

69

Shopping District **58**
Supermarket **66**

Let's Review!

Where do these people work? What are they doing?

Can you describe these tasks the baker needs to do to make and sell baked goods?

allowing the dough to rest	filling the baskets	baking in the electric oven	dividing the dough into equal portions

What does a cheesemonger sell? Why do you think there's a thermometer in the truck?
Can you spot some food items that don't belong in this truck?

These people work in specific types of stores.
Do you know which ones? What do the people do?
What type of store would you like to work at?

Out
and About

Airports and Airplanes

Mechanics, baggage handlers, pilots, flight attendants—thousands of people work at airports and on airplanes around the world.

checking passports
and issuing
boarding passes

ticket agent

checking passengers
and bags for
prohibited items

security officer

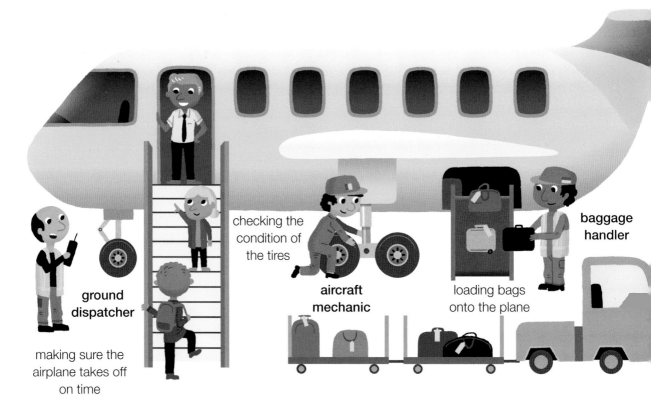

checking the
condition of
the tires

baggage handler

ground dispatcher

aircraft mechanic

loading bags
onto the plane

making sure the
airplane takes off
on time

Flight Deck

When a plane travels through storm clouds, it may shake a lot because of turbulence, a sudden change in air movement.

pilot, or **captain:**
in charge of flying the aircraft

co-pilot:
supports the captain

When there's turbulence, pilots can change the speed of the plane or how high it is in the air to fix the problem.

flight attendants

serving refreshments and explaining safety instructions

guiding airplanes to the gate

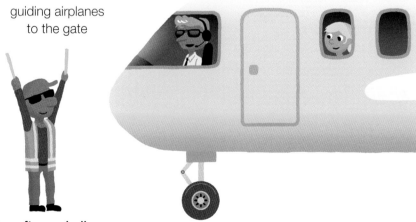

Pilots and the flight crew are prepared to handle many situations. Pilots train on flight simulators to learn to fly in all kinds of weather.

aircraft marshaller

On the Road

When you're traveling on the road, you may see many people hard at work!

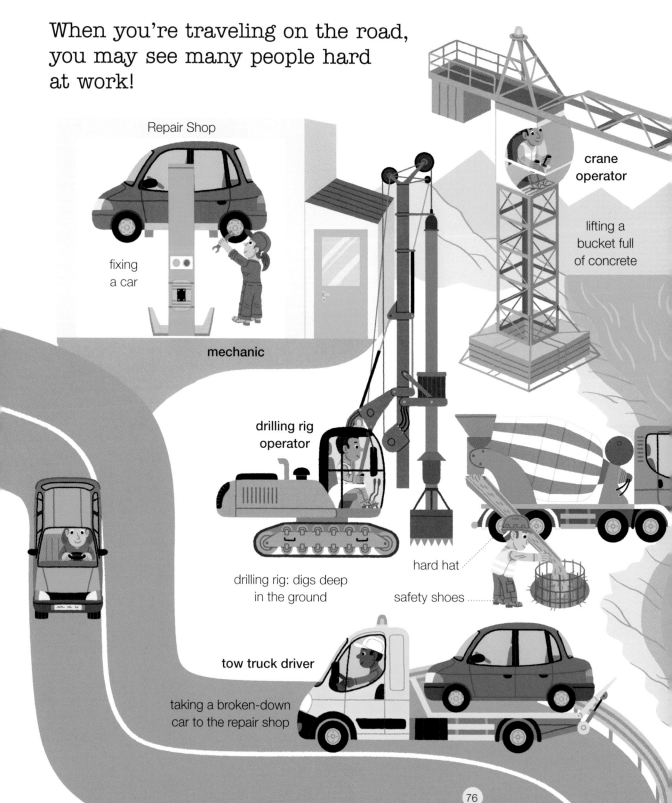

Repair Shop

fixing a car

mechanic

crane operator

lifting a bucket full of concrete

drilling rig operator

drilling rig: digs deep in the ground

hard hat

safety shoes

tow truck driver

taking a broken-down car to the repair shop

Who
builds bridges

There are many types of bridges: arch, suspension, and more. What type of bridge is built depends on the location, the length, and the amount of traffic expected.

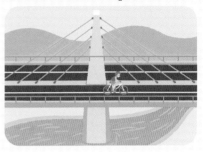

monitoring the speed of cars

police officer

building a bridge pier

concrete worker

welder

using heat to join metal parts together

construction site manager

planning the work schedule and maintaining a safe work site

Architects help design bridges, coming up with a look that will fit in and work with the environment.

They work with civil engineers, who are responsible for the construction of the bridge, making sure that the structure is safe.

At a Restaurant

When dining out, you might see servers bustling around and taking orders, and a host seating people. The kitchen of the restaurant is just as busy!

Kitchen

chef:
in charge of
the kitchen

toque

chef
jacket

sous-chef

placing food
on the plates

sauce chef

preparing
different
sauces

**pastry
chef**

pouring
chocolate

cap

**apprentice
chef**

chopping
vegetables

mandoline

dishwasher

cleaning
the pots

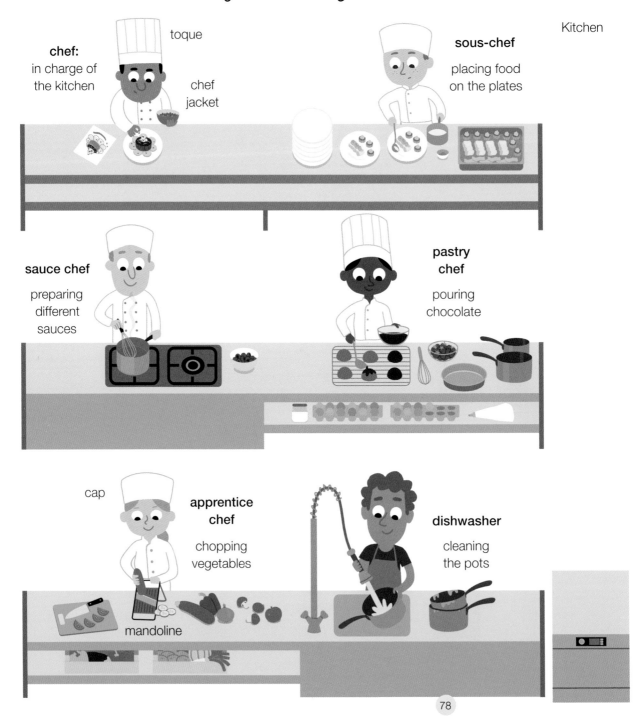

78

Dining Room

head server

setting a table

server

bringing out the food

sommelier

serving wine

server

taking the order

host

greeting the diners

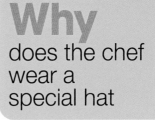

For some jobs, hats can be part of the uniform or worn for safety reasons. Chefs wear hats called toques.

French chef Marie-Antoine Carême invented the toque to help keep chefs' hair from falling into the food. No one likes finding hair in their dinner!

Toques are traditionally white to show how clean the kitchen is. The height of the hat also indicates the chef's rank, so the head chef has the tallest toque!

At the Beach

Here you will find people with all sorts of jobs—lifeguard, beach attendant, paddleboard instructor, and more!

shop manager

selling beach floats

repairing a motor

fish vendor

selling freshly caught fish

marine mechanics

captain tying the boat to the dock

sailor
sorting the fish

paddleboard instructor

checking life jackets

skipper

getting ready for a sailing competition

VISITOR CENTER

offering information to tourists

HOTEL

H

housekeeper

front desk clerk

providing keys to the guests' room

porter

carrying guests' luggage

What
do paddleboard instructors do in the winter ?

When summer ends and the weather turns cold, many paddleboard instructors and those who have beach-related jobs will move on to other jobs.

They may do the same work somewhere else or they may do something different. A paddleboard instructor might give ski lessons in the mountains!

renting out umbrellas

camp counselor

beach attendant

lifeguard

monitoring swimmers

beach vendor

organizing a sandcastle contest

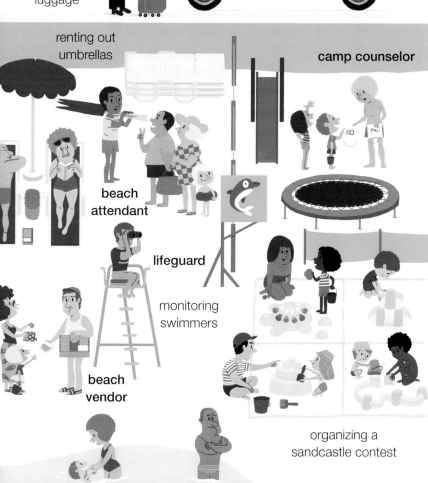

People can have different jobs because of a change in season, or because they need the income. Some people work one job during the day and another at night.

A Zookeeper's Day

Zookeepers spend their day taking care of animals. They have to learn to deal with different kinds of creatures.

morning

preparing meals for the animals

fixing the fences

cleaning up poop

walkie-talkie

calling the veterinarian

examining the tapirs

feeding the penguins

hiding food to keep the lemurs active

cleaning the enclosures

How
dangerous is a zookeeper's job?

afternoon

welcoming
a new llama

weighing
a baby koala

keeping watch
as eggs hatch

putting on a show

evening

feeding the animals

washing the elephant's feet
to remove stones

securing
the enclosures

Zookeepers don't spend their day petting cute baby tigers. They never forget that the animals they care for are wild creatures.

Zookeepers always make sure that they—and zoo visitors—are safe. They use safety equipment such as gloves, boots, and catch poles.

They also conduct drills to prepare for animal escapes, and they always check that the animals' areas are secure.

Museum **38**

🚜 In the Country

Have you ever wondered where some of your food comes from? Here are people on a farm who make that happen.

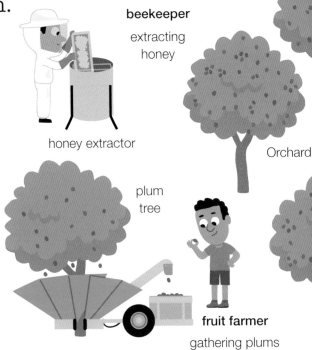

beekeeper

extracting honey

honey extractor

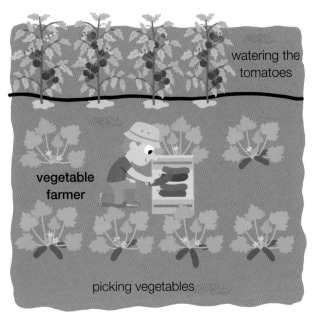

watering the tomatoes

vegetable farmer

picking vegetables

Orchard

plum tree

fruit farmer

gathering plums

farmer

feeding ducks and geese

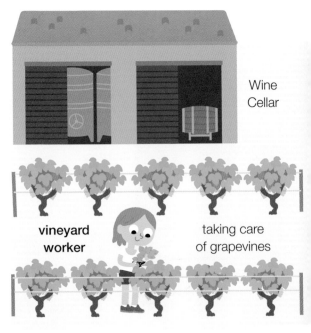

Wine Cellar

vineyard worker

taking care of grapevines

Country Cottage: welcomes visitors

WELCOME TO THE FARM!

selling cheese

milking goats

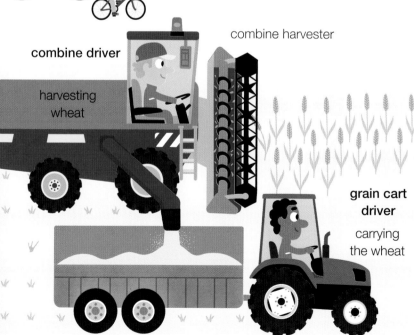

combine harvester

combine driver

harvesting wheat

grain cart driver

carrying the wheat

What does a shepherd do ?

As you hike in the mountains in the summer, you might come across a flock of sheep. They've come to graze on the fresh grass of the high mountain pastures.

The sheep are looked after by shepherds and sheepdogs. They guide the sheep, protect them from predators, and treat their injuries.

Shepherds are hired by sheep ranches to move the flock from one pasture to another. The workers sleep in tents and cabins.

At an Ice Cream Factory

For many people, nothing can taste better on a hot day than ice cream! Who's involved in bringing this delicious treat to everyone? Let's find out!

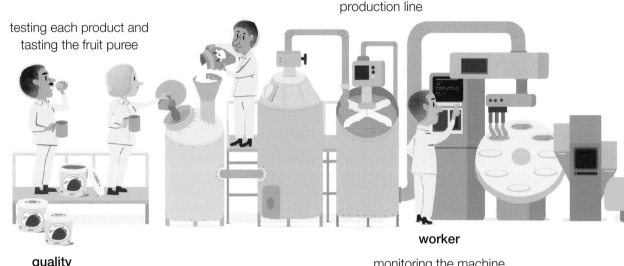

production line

testing each product and tasting the fruit puree

worker

monitoring the machine that fills the tubs

quality controller

marketing team

coming up with possible names for a new ice cream flavor

seeing what customers think

graphic designer

designs the logo

putting the containers
in the freezer

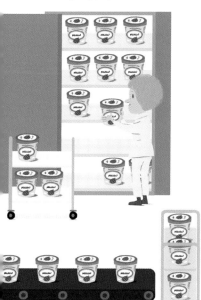

Laboratory

flavorist

mixing flavors and creating
new flavors

Creative Agency

creative team

developing plans to
sell products

If an ice cream commercial made you want to eat ice cream, it did its job well. The commercial was made by an advertising agency.

The agency came up with a slogan or catchphrase that is easy to remember and makes you think of the ice cream.

Next, an actor and a director were hired to film the commercial. Then the commercial was edited and music was added, making it ready to show on TV!

A Baker's Day **64**
At a Restaurant **78**

In the Mountains

There are people whose job is to protect nature.

animal photographer

wearing camouflage

forest manager

marking trees to be cut so other plants can grow

lumberjack

cutting down a tree

nature activity leader

Sawmill

logger

selling wood

showing children how to observe little creatures

mountain
guide

taking a group
on a trail

Observatory

ornithologist

observing
birds

astronomer

Nature
Park

studying space, including
stars and planets

ranger

checking fishing
permits

hydrobiologist

collecting a water
sample

Do you like learning about
space, stars, and planets?
You might want to be an
astronomer or an astronaut.

While astronauts go to space,
astronomers study space from
Earth, using high-powered
telescopes to observe planets
and stars.

Astronauts train for space
missions and study the effects of
space on their bodies and other
living things. They also learn to
deal with weightlessness.

Let's Review!

Observe this zookeeper's activities.
Why is he weighing the baby koala? What are the penguins eating?
What's happening in the scene with the tapirs? Why is he cutting up apples?

What are the names of the jobs that these people have?
Where do they work? Do you know what they are doing?

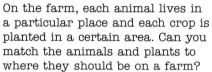

On the farm, each animal lives in a particular place and each crop is planted in a certain area. Can you match the animals and plants to where they should be on a farm?

Where does this scene take place? What's going on? Who is standing by the door at the front of the plane?

Index

DO YOU KNOW?™ series

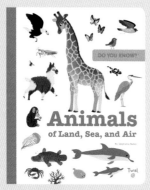

978-2-40803-356-9

978-2-40802-467-3

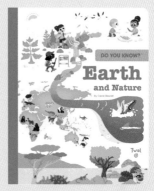

978-2-40803-357-6

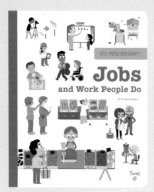

978-2-40803-753-6

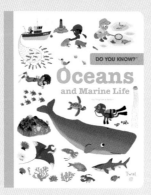

978-2-40802-466-6

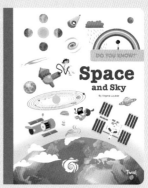

978-2-40802-916-6

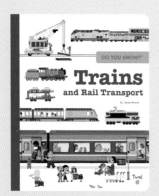

978-2-40803-755-0

978-2-40802-915-9